WaShington DOODLES

Illustrated and Written by John Skewes

SASQUATCH BOOKS
SEATTLE

Text and illustrations copyright © 2010 by John Skewes
All rights reserved. No portion of this book may be reproduced or utilized in any form, or by any electronic, mechanical, or other means, without the prior written permission of the publisher.

Manufactured in the United States of America by Bang Printing (Minnesota), in June 2010
Published by Sasquatch Books
Distributed by PGW/Perseus

16 15 14 13 12 11 10   10 9 8 7 6 5 4 3 2 1

Book design by Sarah Plein

Skewes, John.
  Washington doodles: over 200 doodles to create your own Evergreen State / written and illustrated by John Skewes.
      p. cm.
  ISBN-13: 978-1-57061-666-2
  ISBN-10: 1-57061-666-3
1. Doodles--Juvenile literature. 2. Washington (State)--Juvenile literature. 3. Drawing books. I. Title.
II. Title: Over 200 doodles to create your own Evergreen State. III. Title: Over two hundred doodles to create your own Evergreen State.
  NC915.D6S59 2010
  741--dc22
                                        2010019997
Sasquatch Books
119 South Main Street, Suite 400
Seattle, WA 98104
(206) 467-4300
www.sasquatchbooks.com
custserv@sasquatchbooks.com

SPRING

What does Washington make you think of?

Fill the tree with apples.

Don't step in the mud puddles!

Draw the caterpillars eating the leaves.

What did the
sea lion eat?

Draw the view from the ferry boat.

Draw the people in the bus.

Add your own sculptures
to the park.

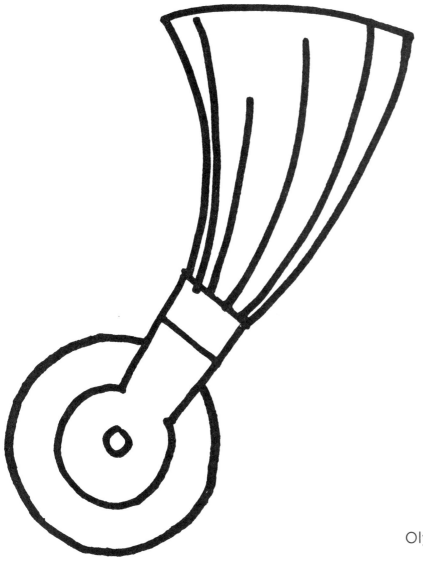

Olympic Sculpture Park, Seattle

Draw a waterfall.

Draw a river (or rivers) through the woods.

Color the totem poles.

The sea lion wants to eat the salmon.
Can you draw something to stop him?

Draw all the birds flying over the water.

Draw all the boats on the water.

Draw all the fish under the water.

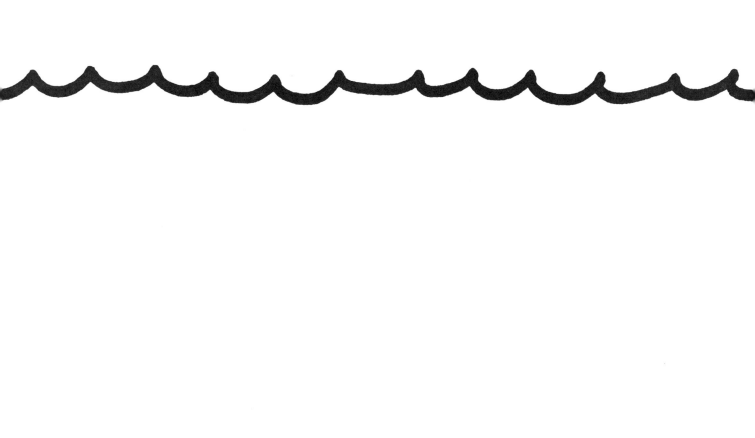

Draw petals for the flowers.

Draw a web for the spider.

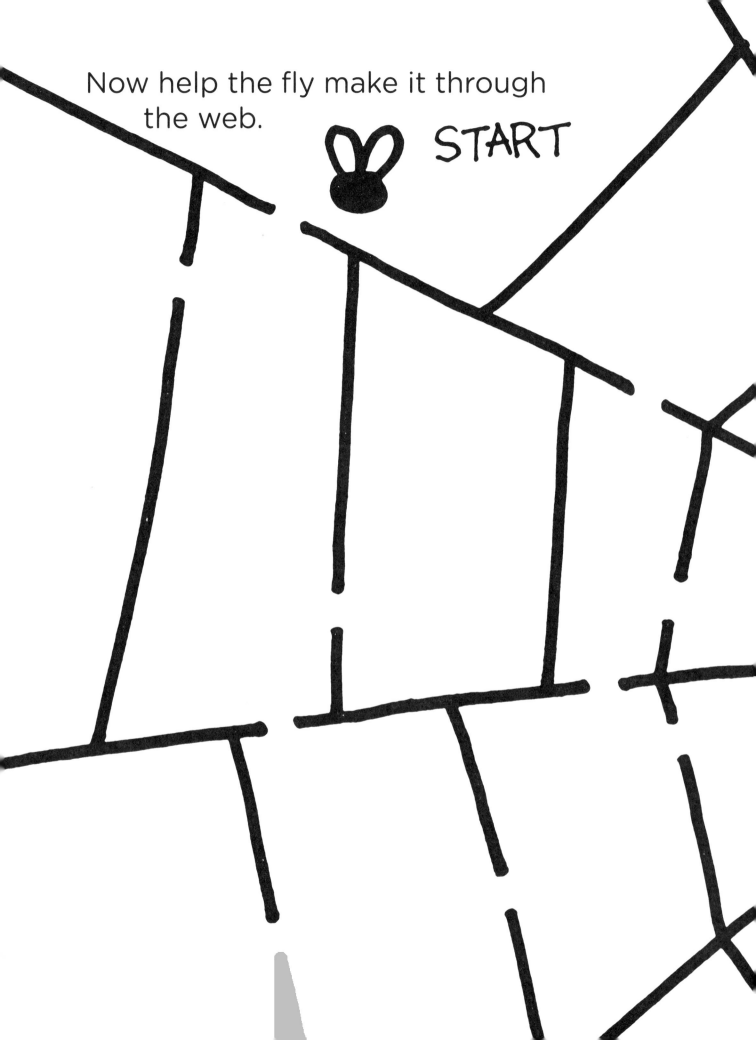

Now help the fly make it through the web.

START

FINISH

The scuba diver is feeding the fish in the aquarium.

This truck is hauling logs.

Draw all the people swimming in
Puget Sound.

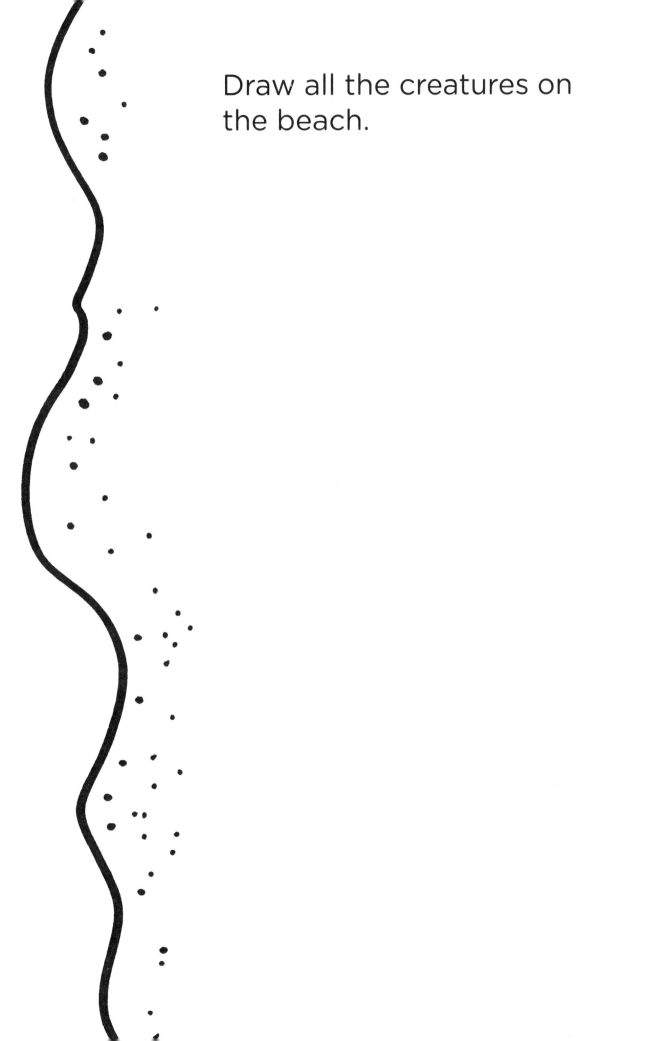

Draw all the creatures on the beach.

What time is it at Pike Place Market?

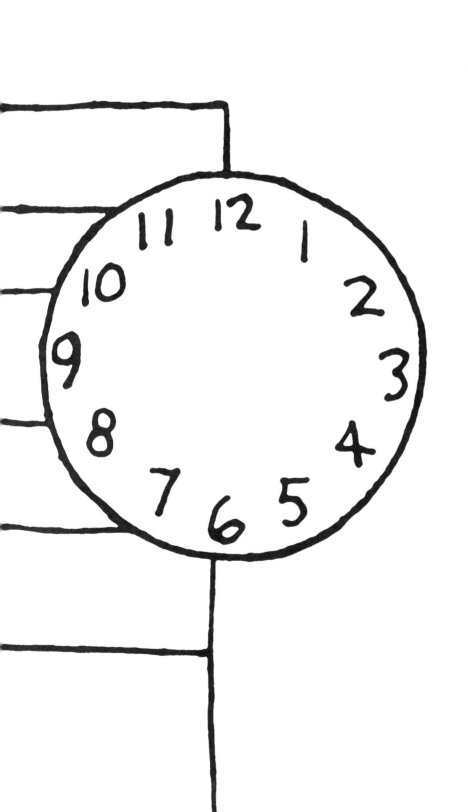

PACIFIC
OCEAN

Can you connect the Columbia River
to the Pacific Ocean?

COLUMBIA RIVER

At Pike Place Market they toss salmon.
Draw the fish!

What grows in your garden?

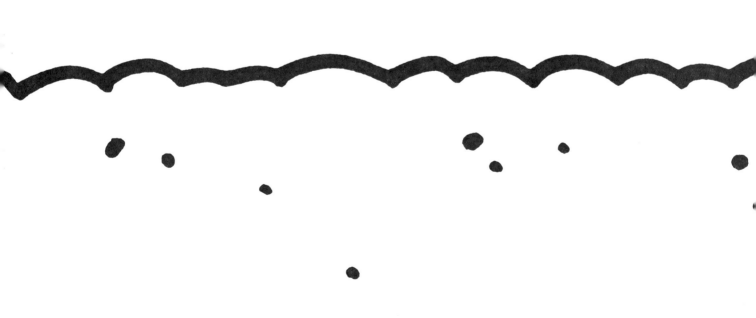

Who is eating the garden?

How many turtles are on the log?

Can you dig your way to the clam?

Draw the seagulls on the pilings.

Draw crows on the wires.

Can you fill all the bins with fruit at
Pike Place Market?

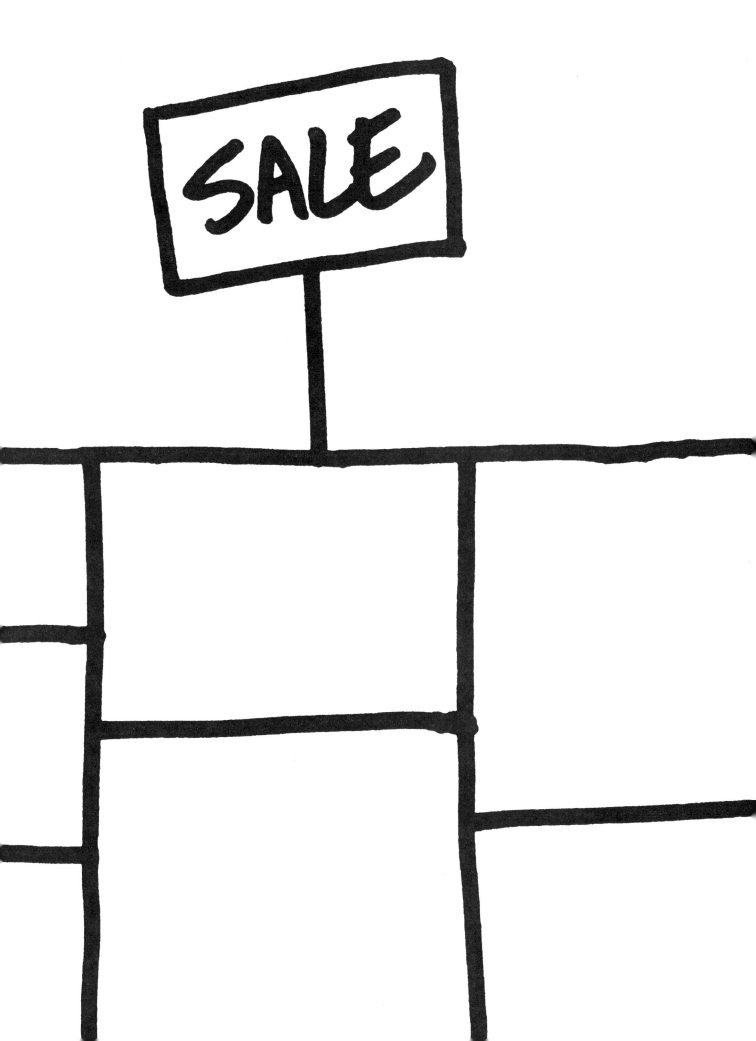

Fill the ferry boat with cars and people.

Color the rainbow.

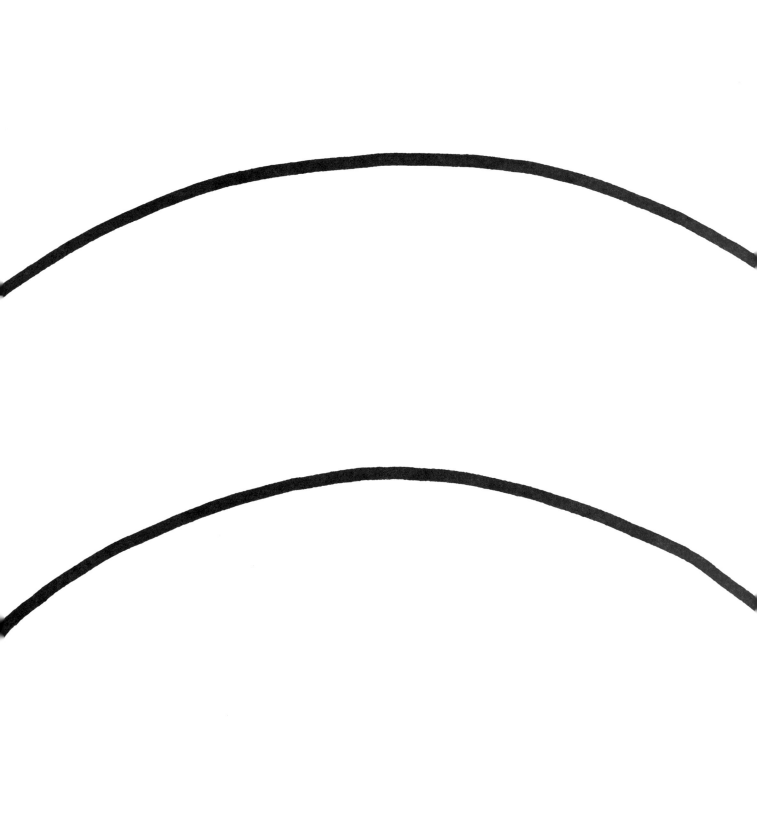

Washington State is named for President Washington. Look at a dollar and draw him.

WASHINGTON

ONE DOLLAR

Now draw yourself on the dollar.

ONE DOLLAR

What will you buy with your dollar?

Draw all the cars on Interstate 5.

What is trying to eat the fish?

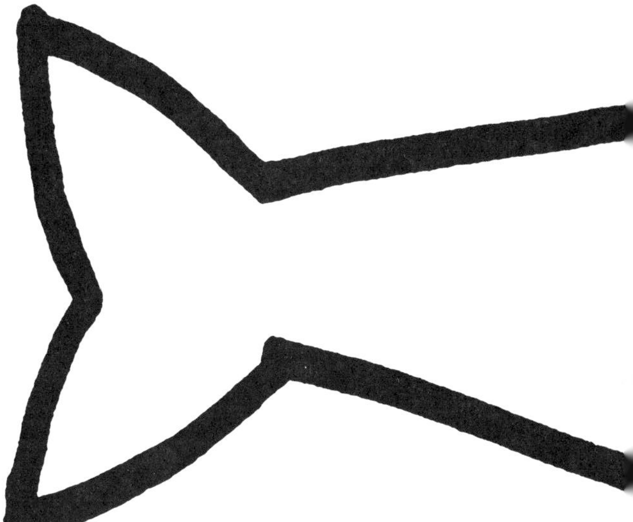

Is the Fremont Bridge open or closed?

Draw a spring day.

Draw all the walkers, runners, and bikers around Green Lake.

Draw the row boats and swimmers in Green Lake.

Draw the mountain bikers riding uphill.

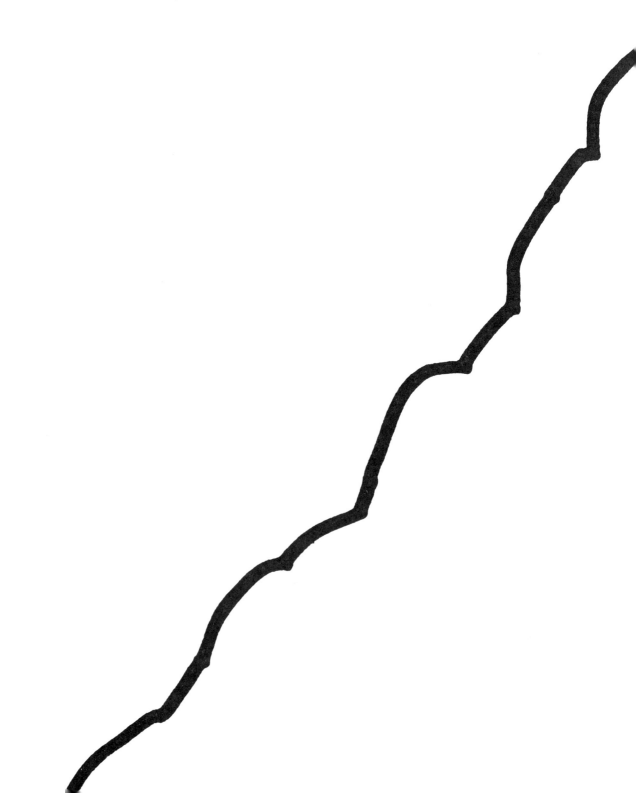

It's easier on the way down.

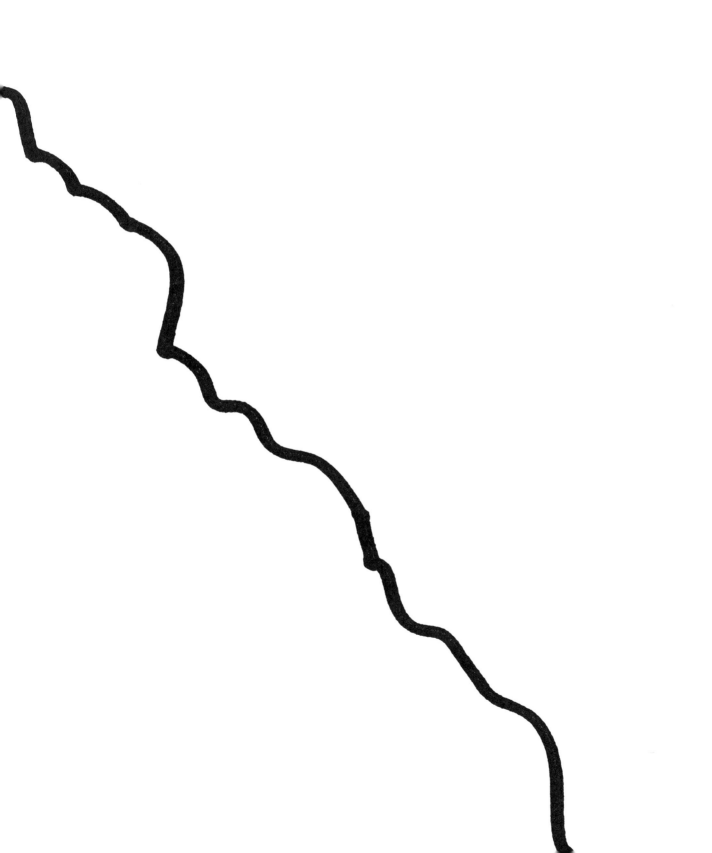

Boeing builds airplanes. Fill the sky with planes!

Draw the floats in the Seafair Parade.

Draw Fourth of July
fireworks over the city.

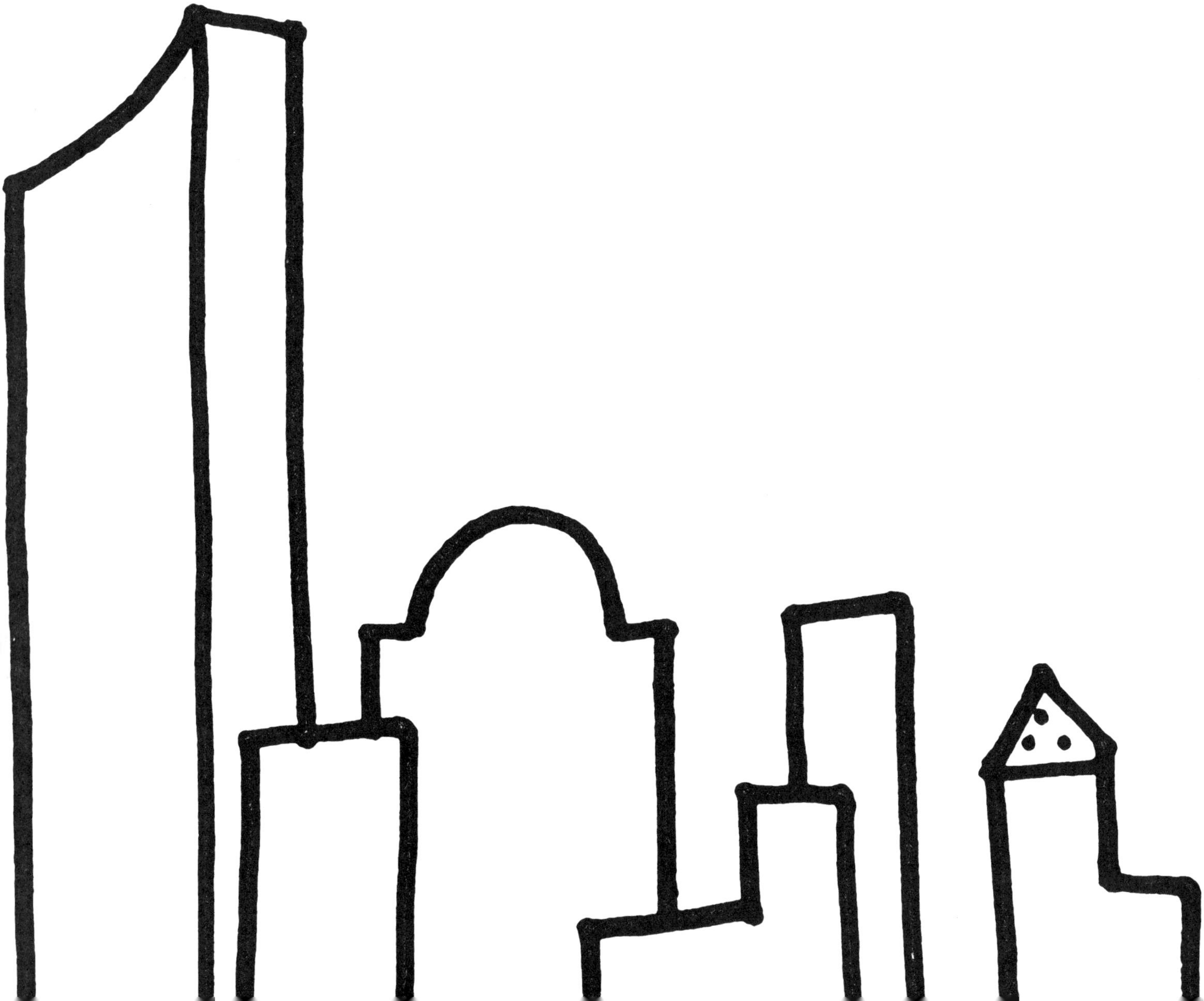

You made the front page of the newspaper!

The Seattle Times

What's the headline?

Finish the log cabin.

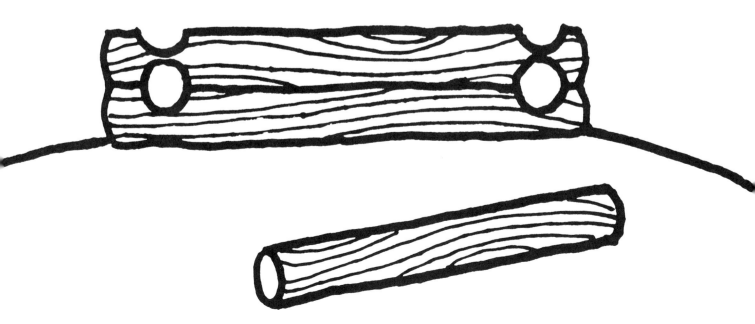

Help Pete find his dog, Larry.

Color the spinnaker sail.

Now draw the wind.

Draw a cowboy on the horse.

Draw a horse under the cowboy.

It's a hydroplane race! Draw the other hydroplanes.

Draw the boats going through
Ballard Locks.

Now draw the salmon jumping up the fish ladder.

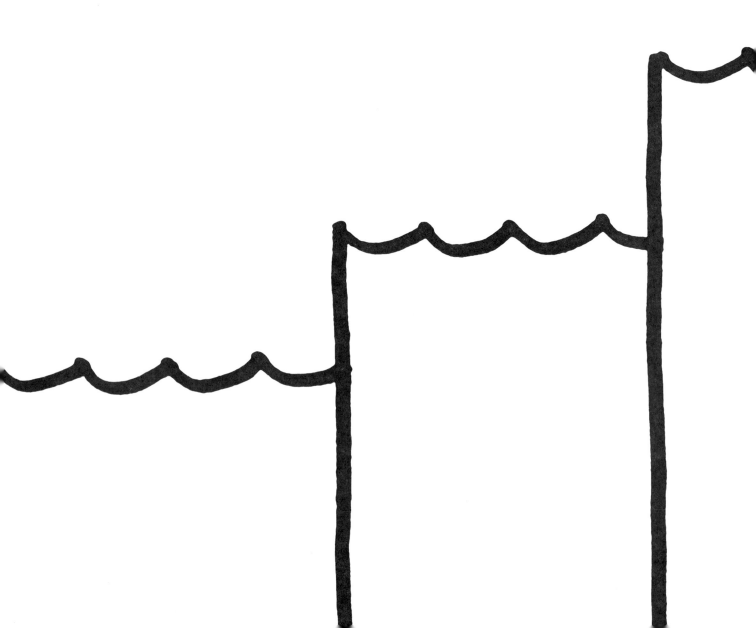

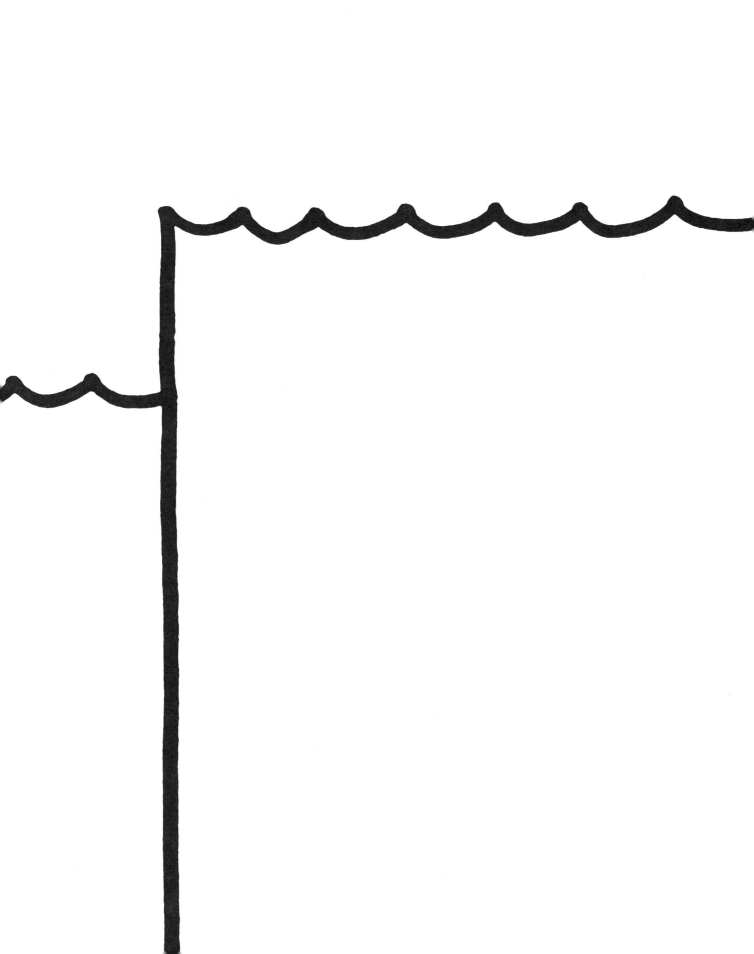

Color the "Ride the Ducks" vehicle. Fill it with people.

Now put it in the water!

The Mariners are playing in Safeco Field.
Draw the players.

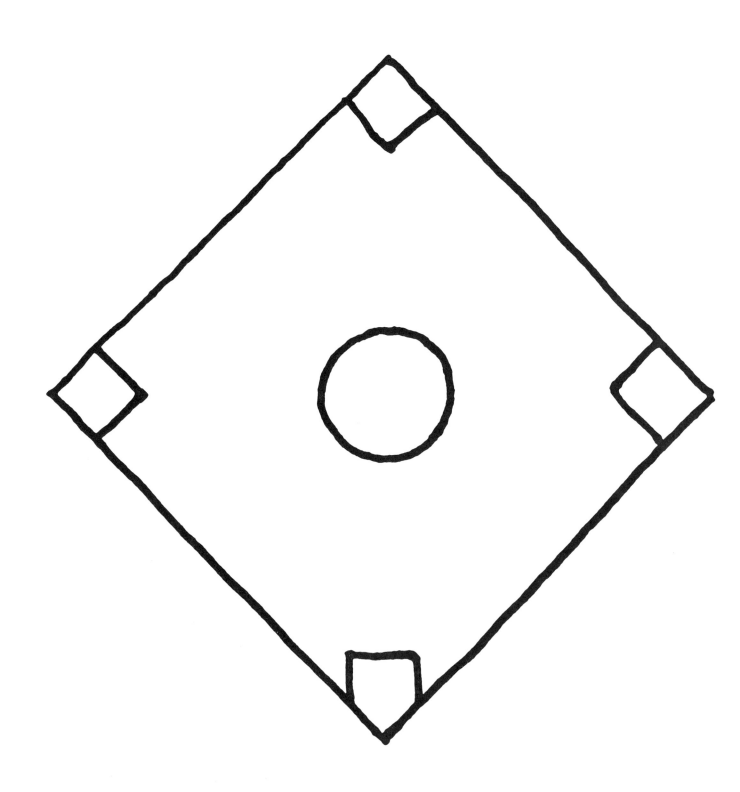

Now draw the fans.

Who is under the water?

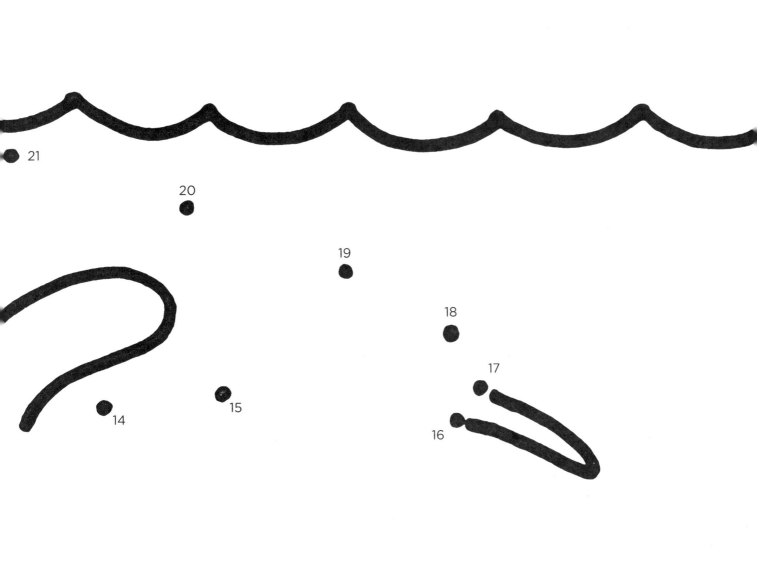

21

20

19

18

17

16

15

14

Draw all the bikes on the bike path.

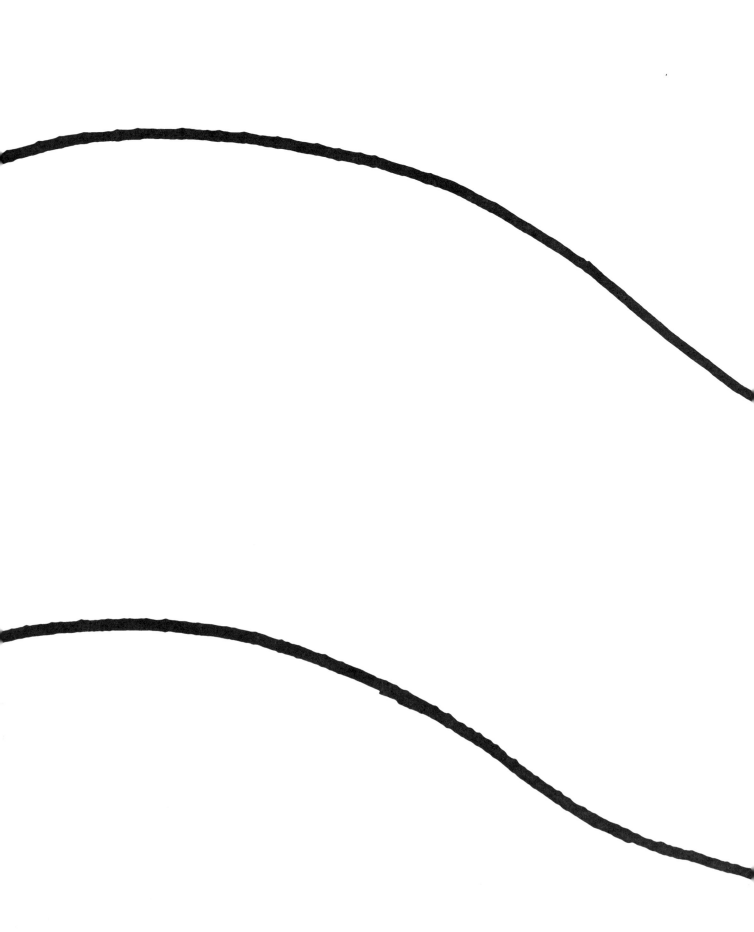

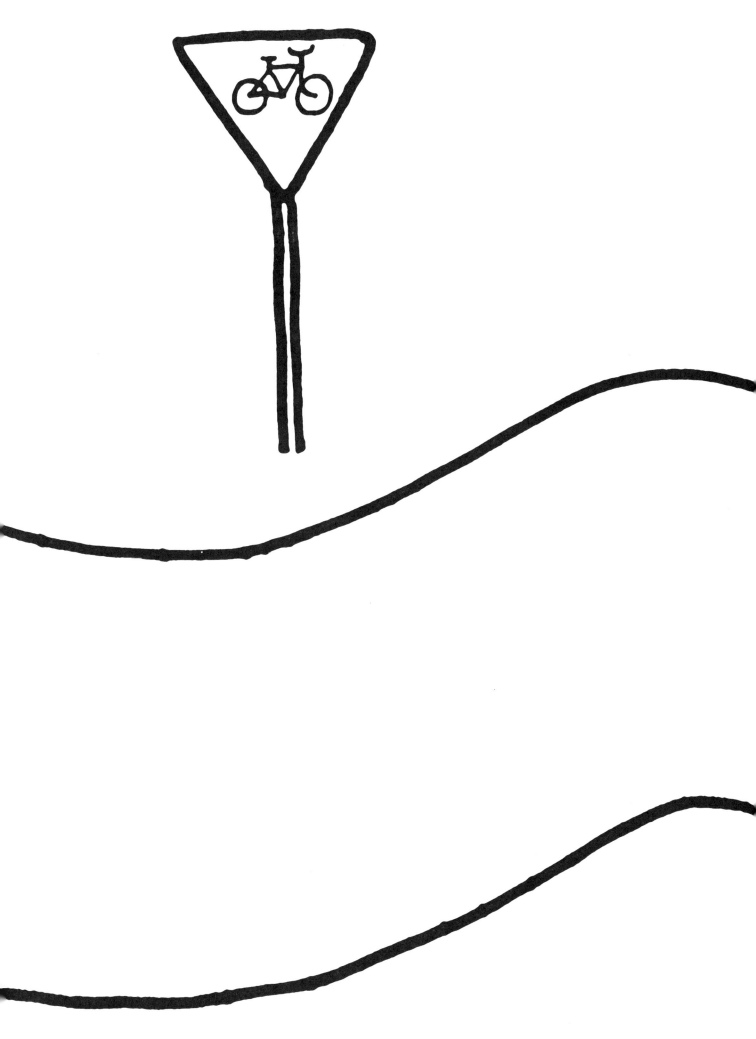

Tie the boat to the dock so it won't float away.

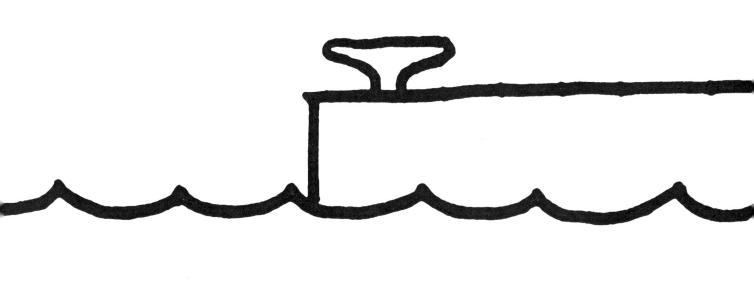

How many boats are tied to the dock?

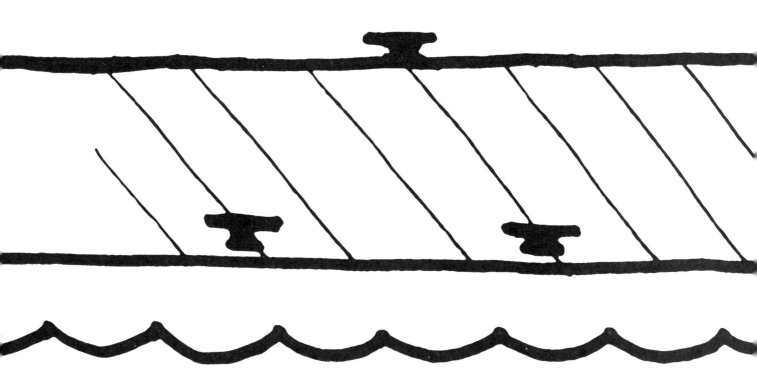

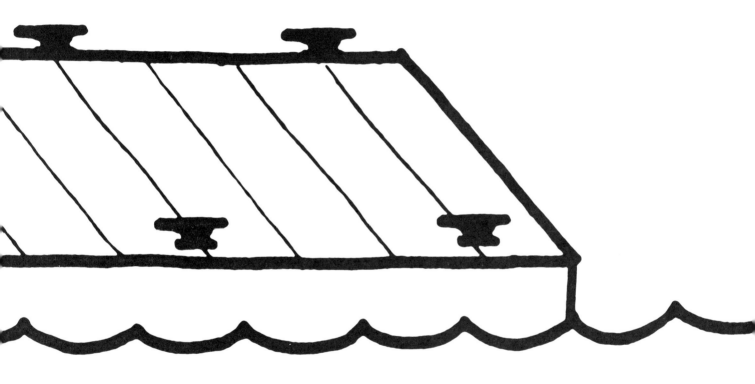

Draw tattoos!

More tattoos!

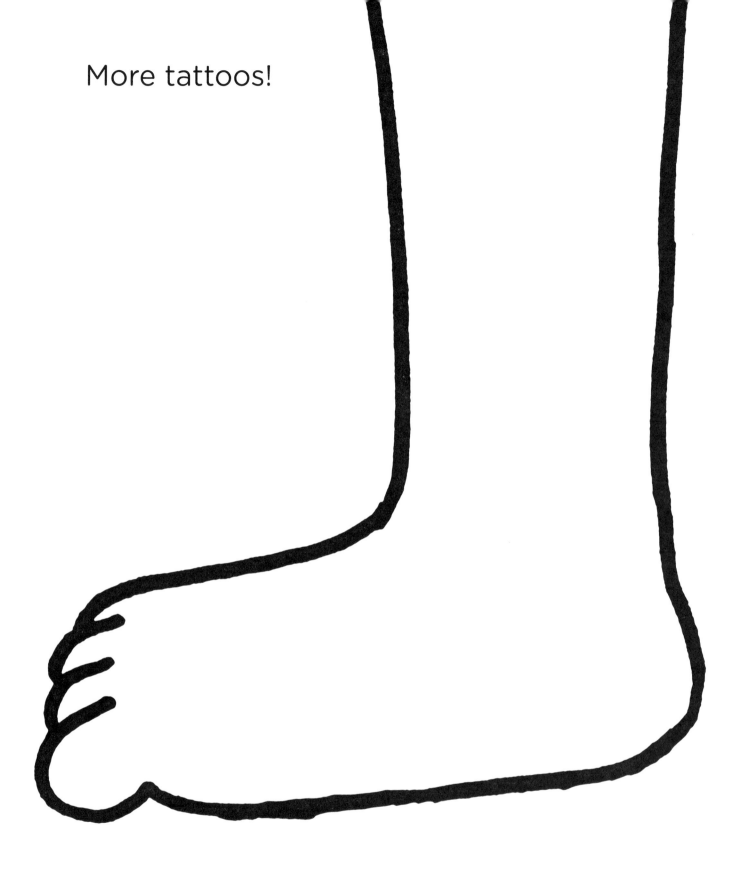

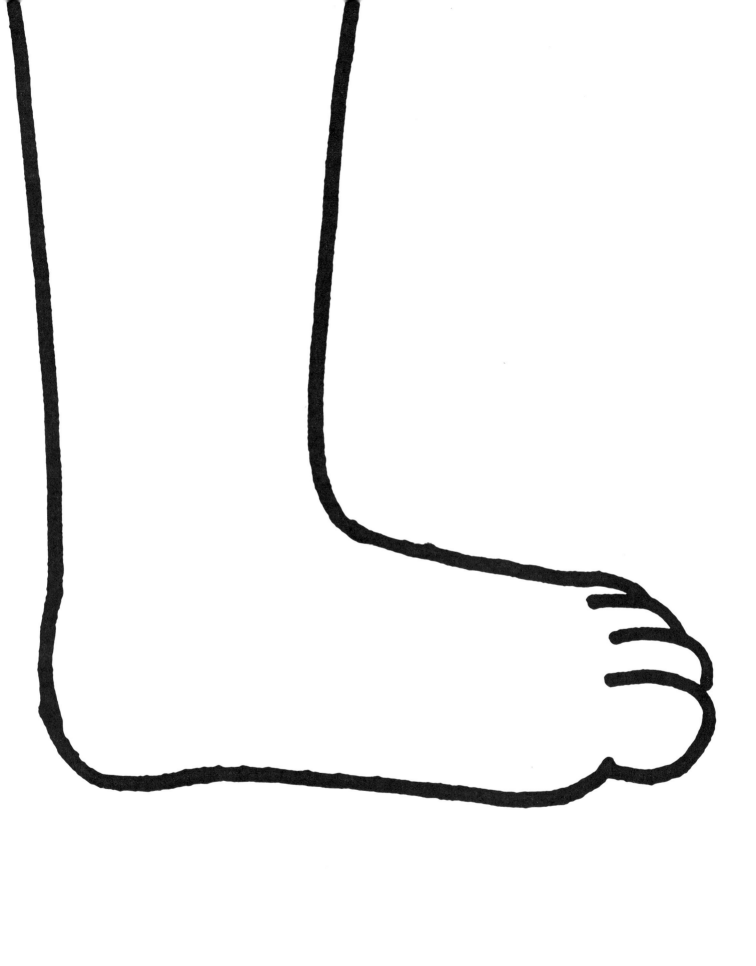

Danny and Debbie hear noises outside the tent when they are camping. What's out there?

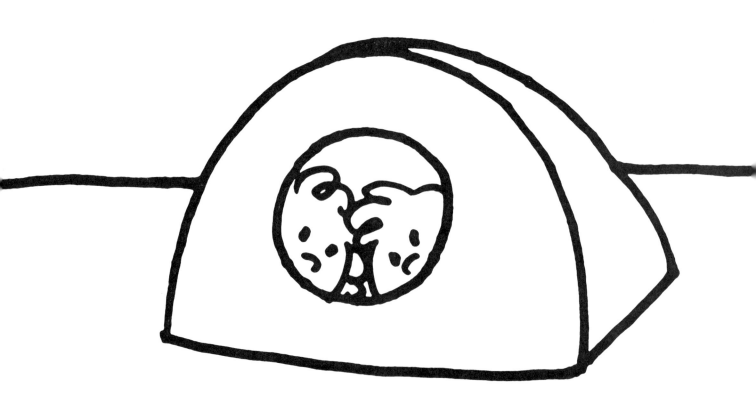

This slide looks like a giant wagon.
Draw the children sliding down.

Riverfront Park, Spokane

Draw the Monorail.

Two men are having a log rolling contest.
One wins.

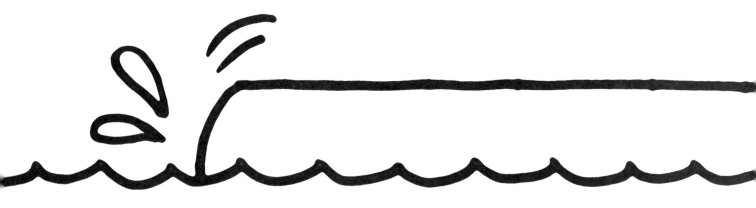

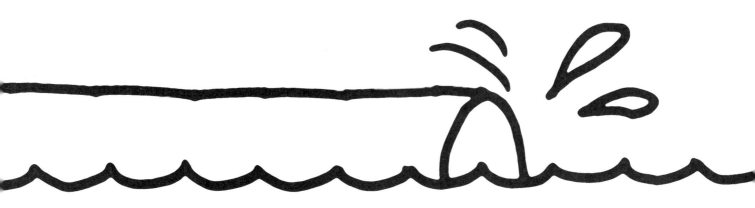

One loses.

Draw someone kicking the soccer ball.

Connect the dots to see who's behind the mask.

Draw a cow for the farmer to milk.

Draw the Seafair Princess.

Draw the water skier behind the boat.

What is the glass blower making?

Draw the animals in the zoo.

Draw the boy's kite.

Draw a picture here . . .

Now cut it out and
mail it to a friend.

fold

STAMP

fold

fold

glue

What shape is Debbie's balloon?

Draw a summer day.

FALL

Draw the quarterback throwing the football.

Draw a receiver to catch it.

Draw the boats in the sailboat race.
Which one will win?

Connect the sailor to the knot.

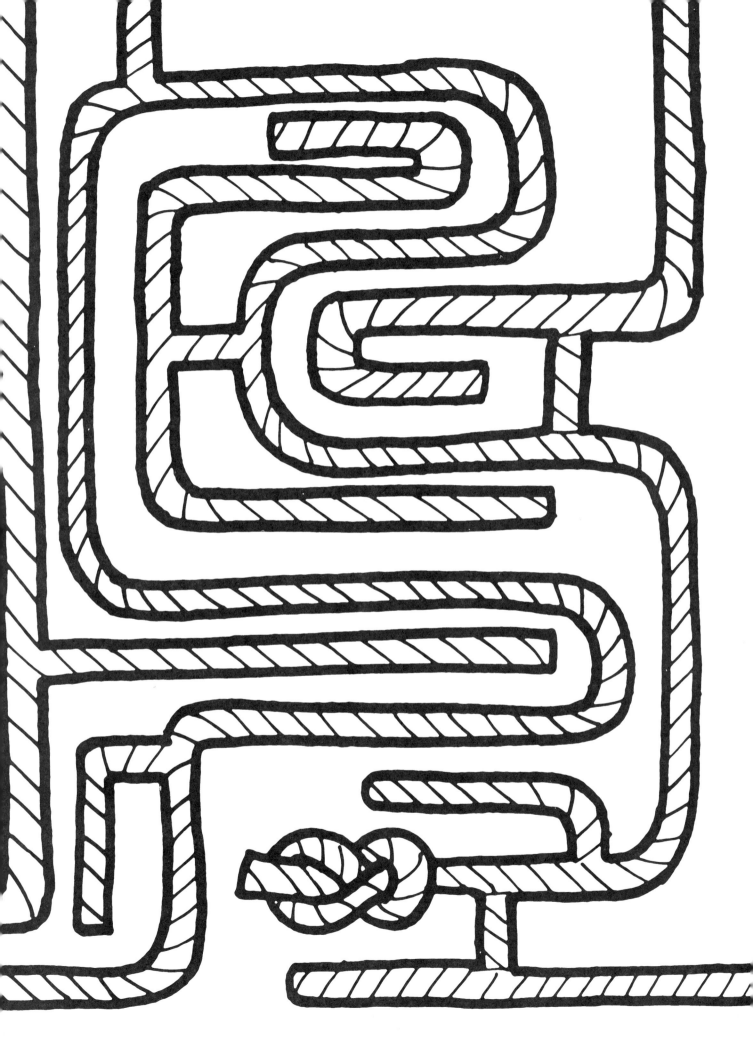

It's autumn. Draw all the colorful leaves on the tree.

Now draw them on the ground.

These are pine branches.
Draw pinecones and pine needles.

This is Mount Rainier.
Who is climbing it?

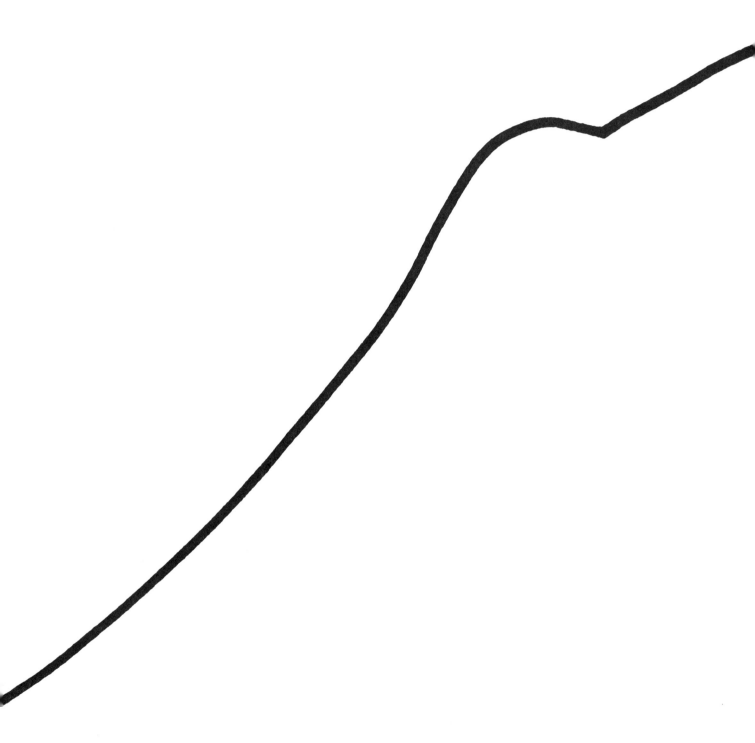

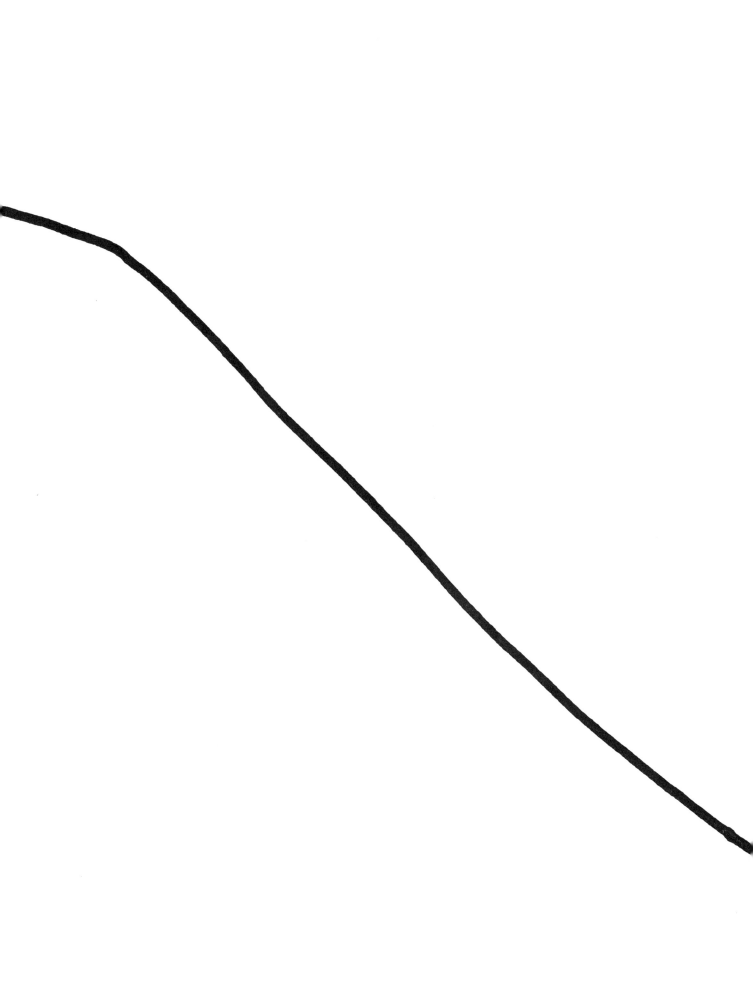

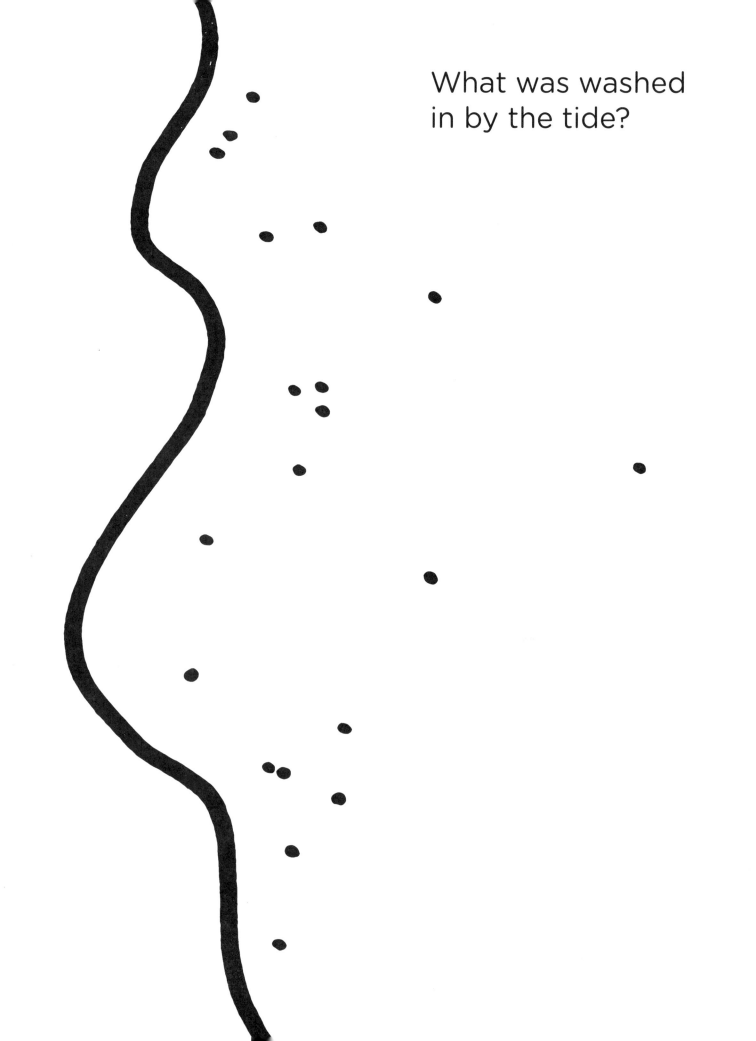

What was washed
in by the tide?

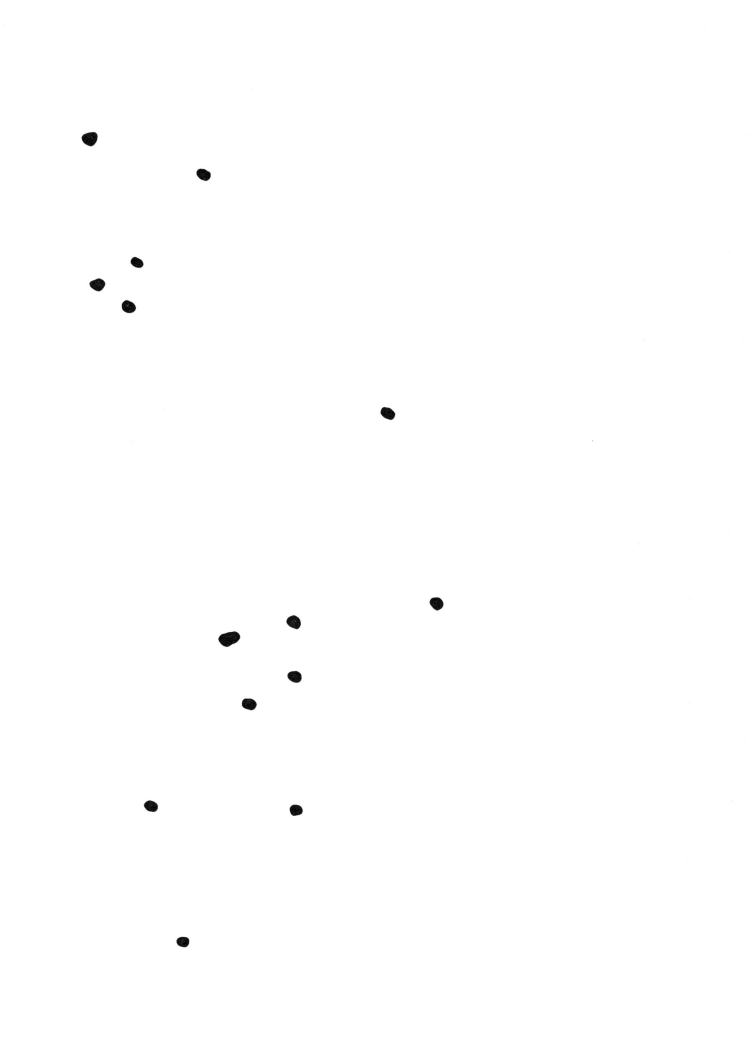

Fill the pumpkin patch.

Draw a face on the pumpkin.

Draw a cup of coffee in this person's hand.

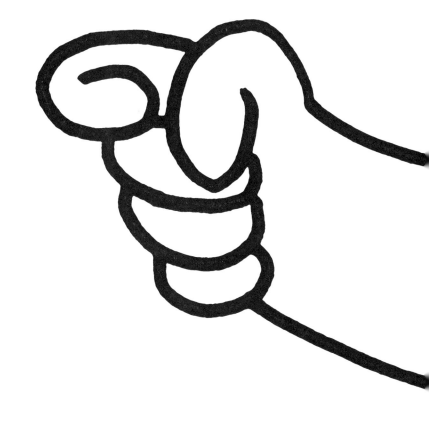

Where is Bigfoot walking? Draw his footprints.

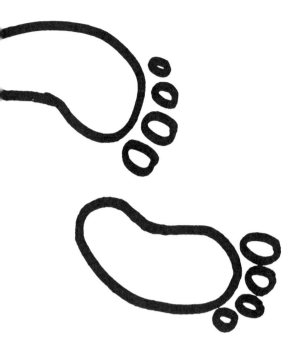

How many cows are
in the pasture?

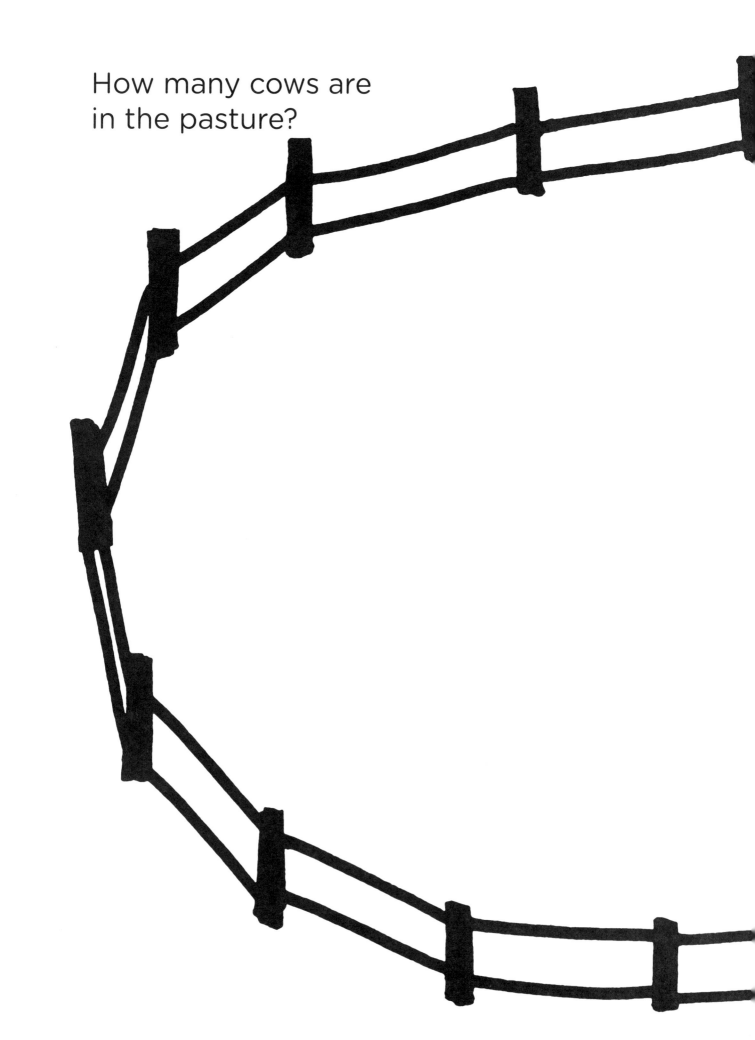

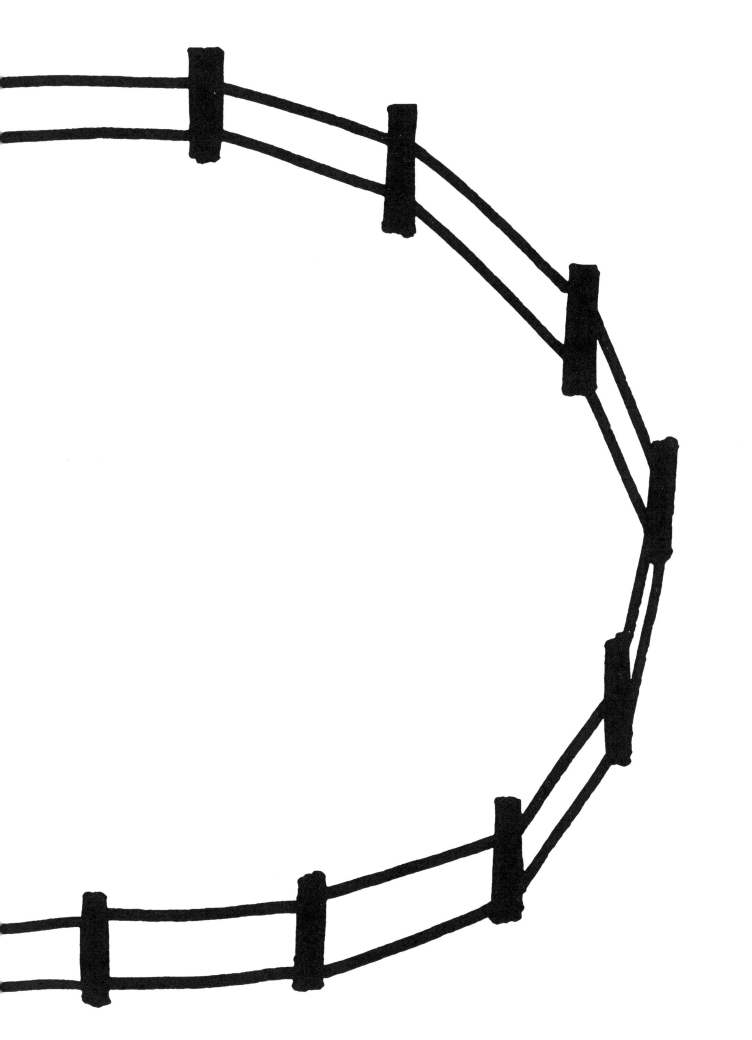

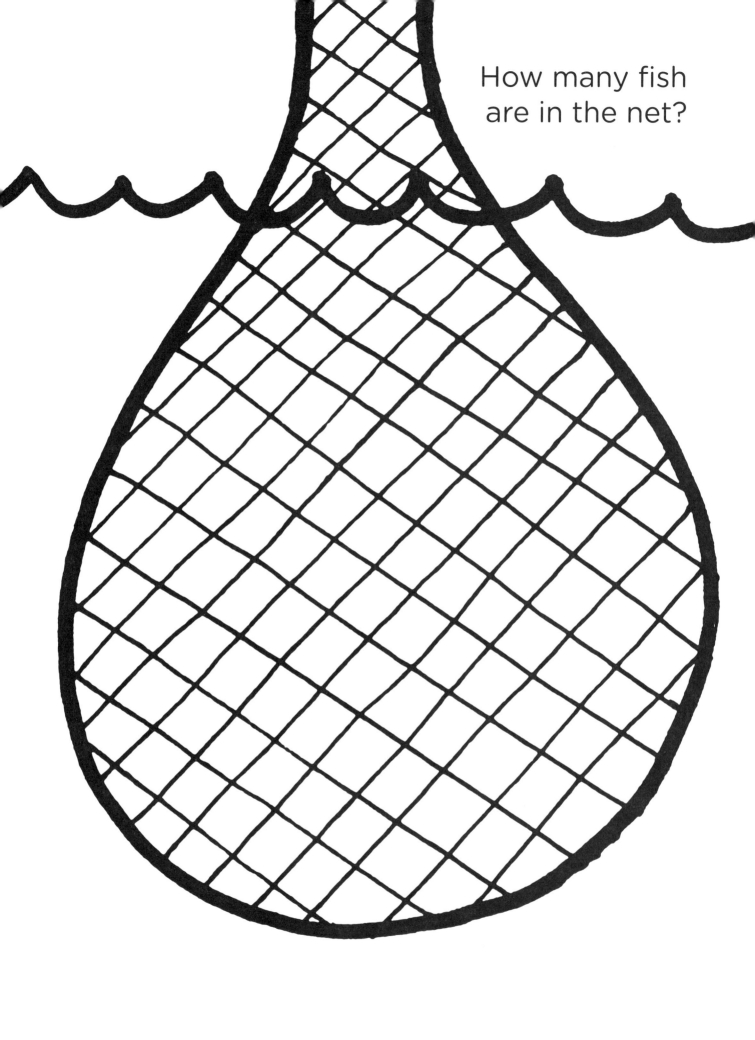

How many fish
are in the net?

Draw faces on the totem pole.

Color the falling leaves.

Can you draw eight legs on the octopus?

Who is crossing the floating bridge?

Draw a Husky.

Draw a Cougar.

Who's wearing the rain boots?

Who's landing at Sea-Tac Airport?

What's in the barge?

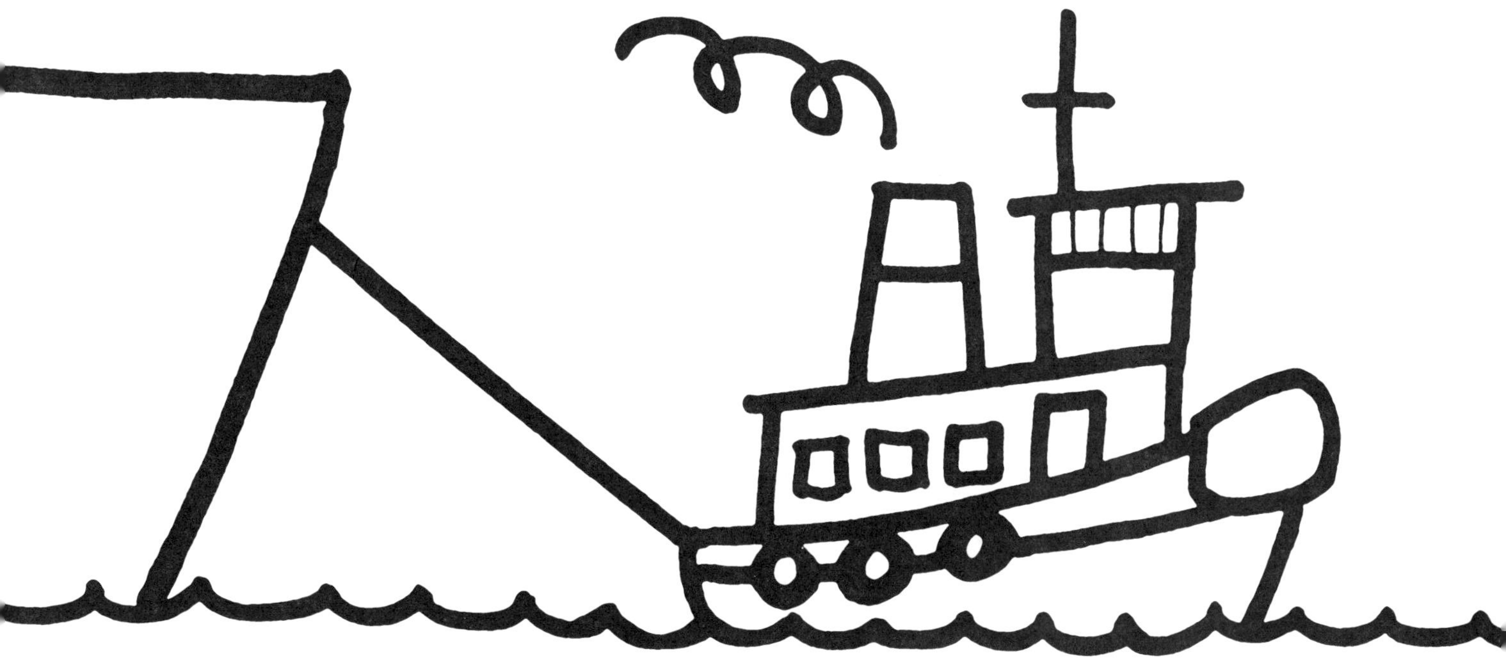

Make a hiking trail for Danny and Debbie.

Who is sitting in the tree?

Now draw his friends.

Draw something big.

Draw something small.

Build a bridge across the
Tacoma Narrows.

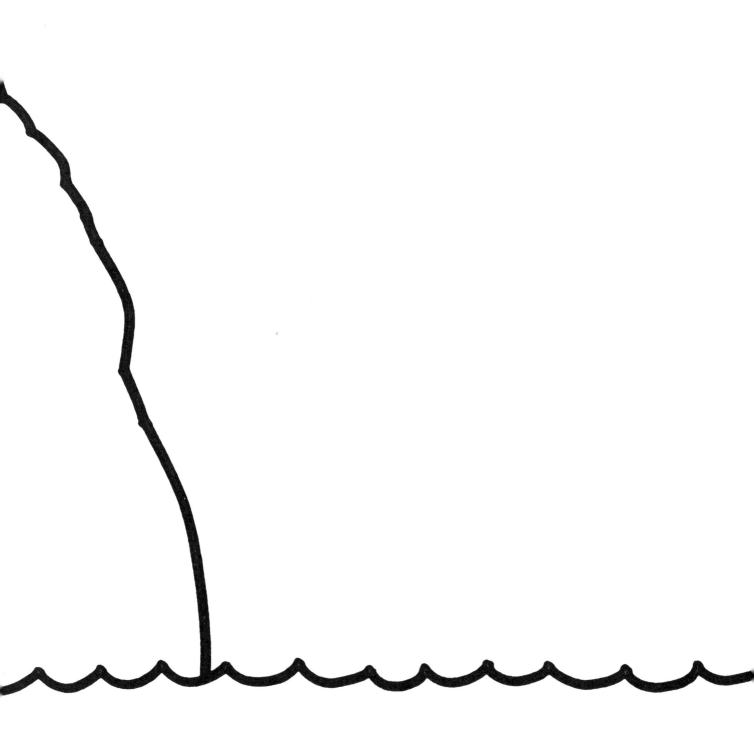

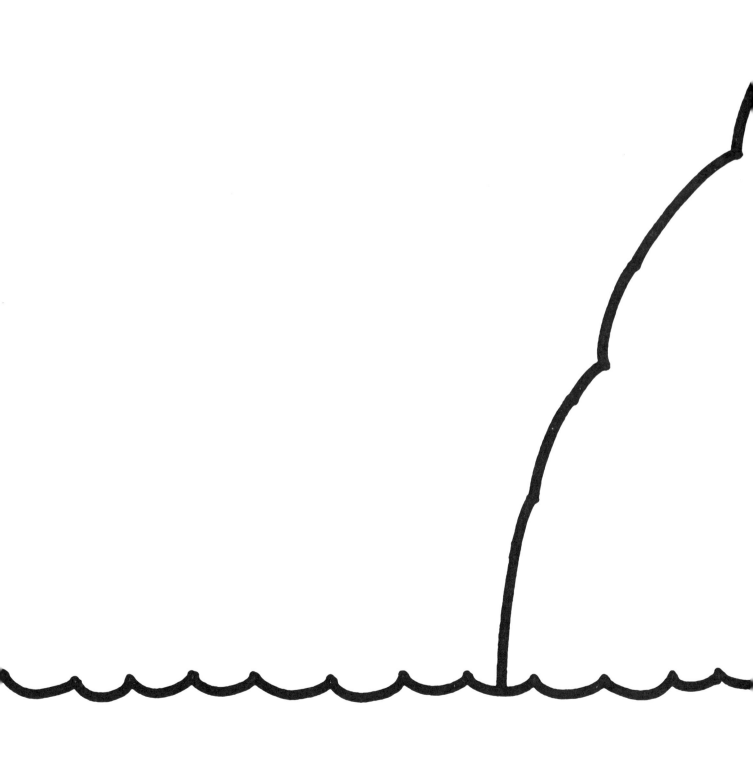

Who is jumping in the mud puddle?

Who is holding the umbrella?

Ick! Draw the trail of the slug.

What can you make out of the clouds?

Draw the policeman's uniform.

Draw the fireman's uniform.

Draw the band.

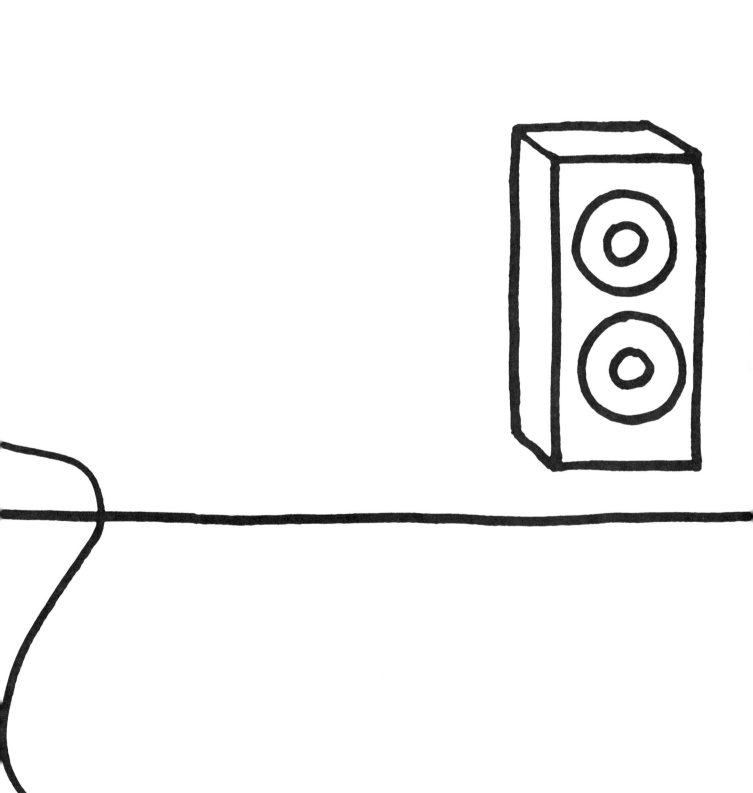

Help the fireboat put out the fire.

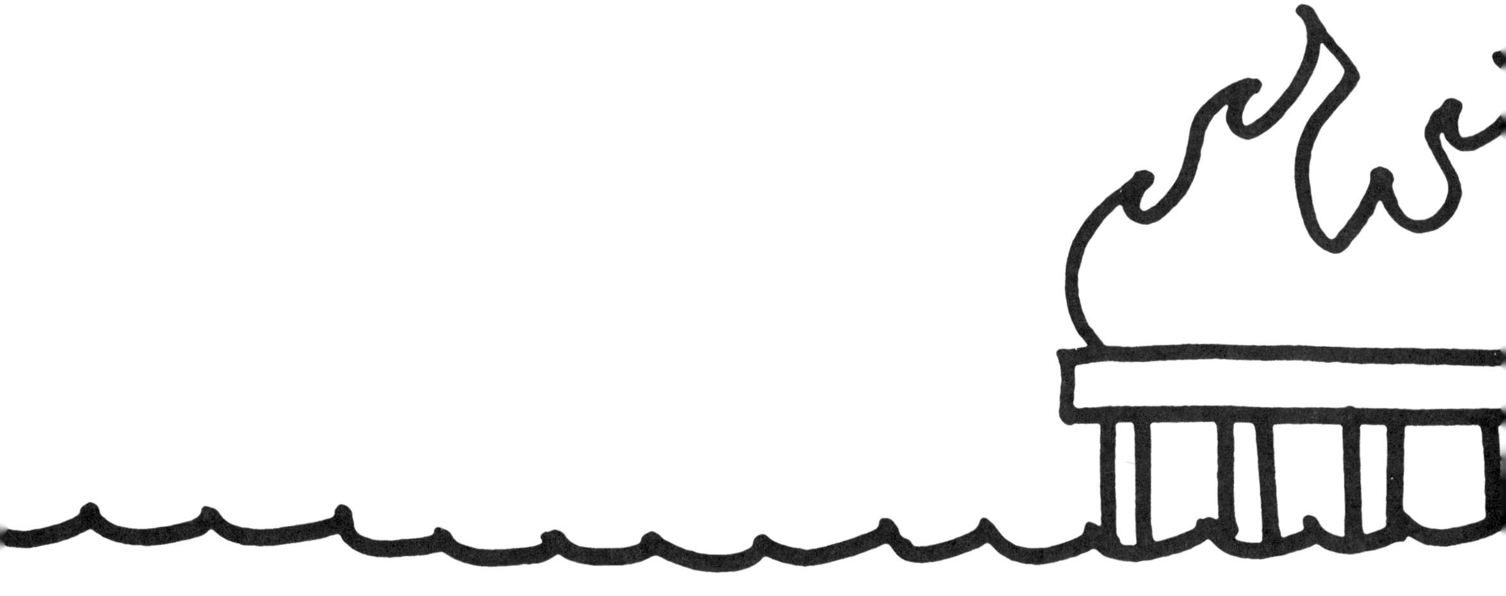

Make a mountain bike trail for
Danny and Debbie.

Draw hats on the Seafair Pirates.

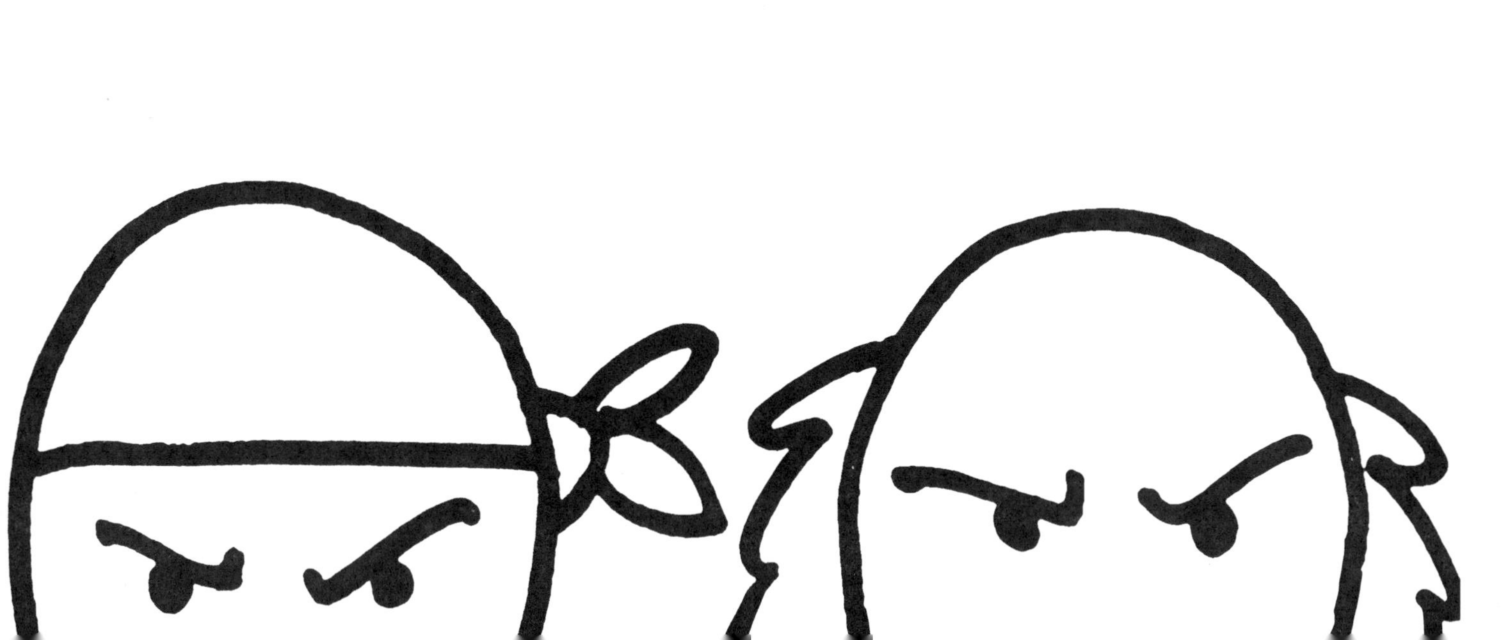

Draw something

very,

very,

very,

very

small.

Where is the elevator going? Connect the dots.

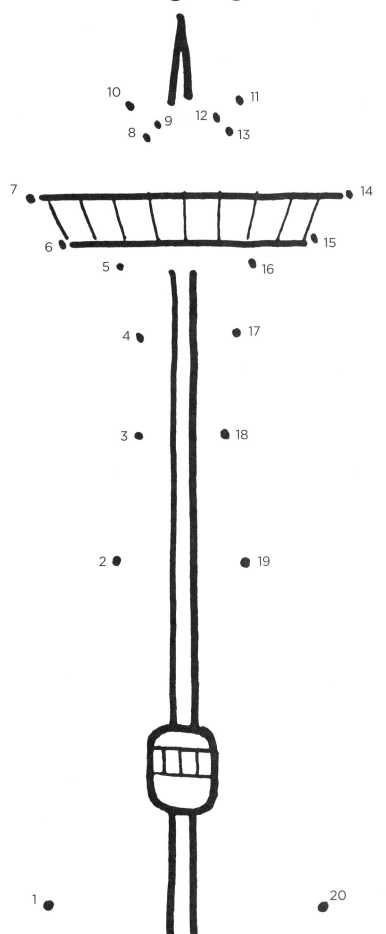

Draw antlers on the moose.

Color the frog.

Color the toad.

Give the orca teeth.

What did the heron catch in its bill?

Draw the antlers on the deer.

A bear is scratching his back against the tree.

A bear left this track.

Draw the bear.

Draw a fall day.

WINTER

Draw the skiers' trails.

Draw holiday lights on the Space Needle.

Snow covered everything. What's under the snow?

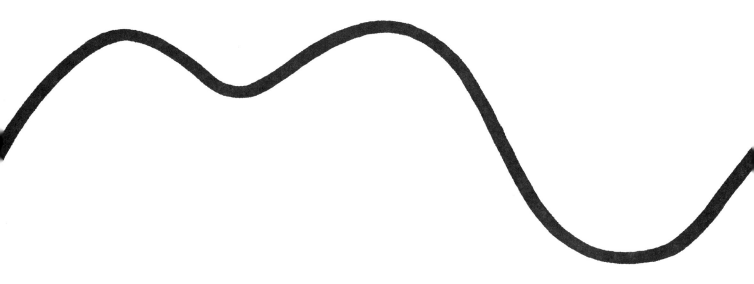

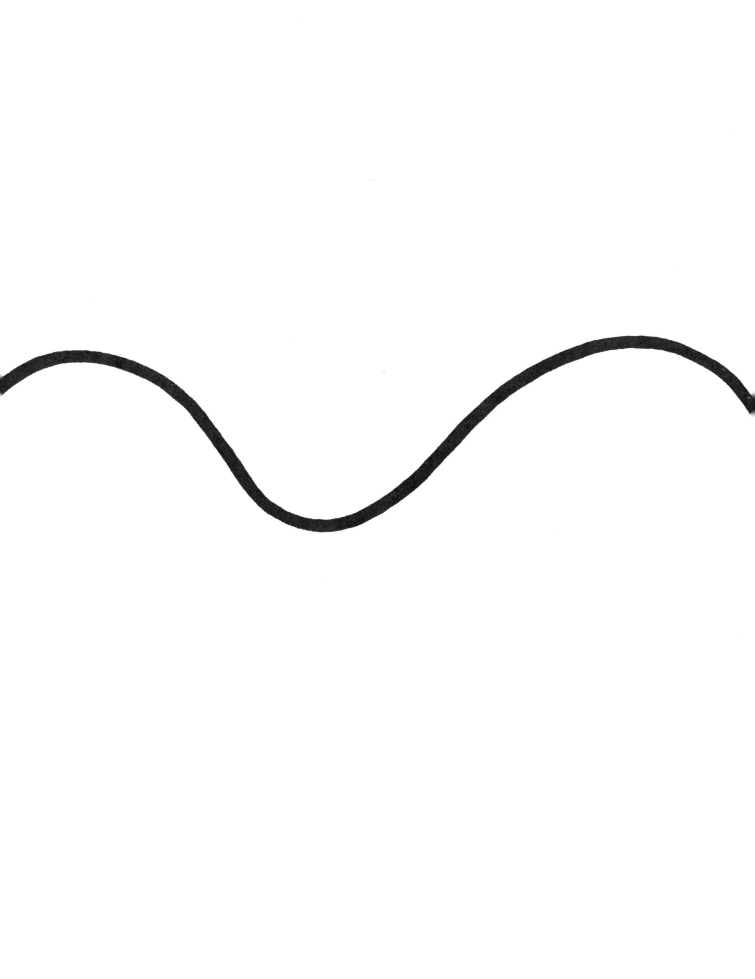

This is Danny. Draw his winter clothes.

This is Debbie. Draw her winter clothes.

It's cold outside! Color Debbie's hat, scarf, and mittens.

Color Danny's boots and socks.

It's snowing now. Are they happy or sad?

Now it's raining.

And raining, and raining...

It's freezing! Draw icicles on the roof.

Now build a snowman.

Draw the winter hats and coats hanging on the hooks.

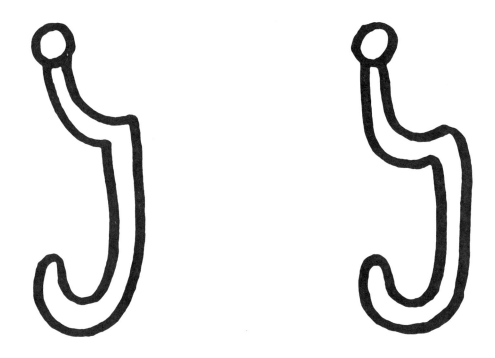

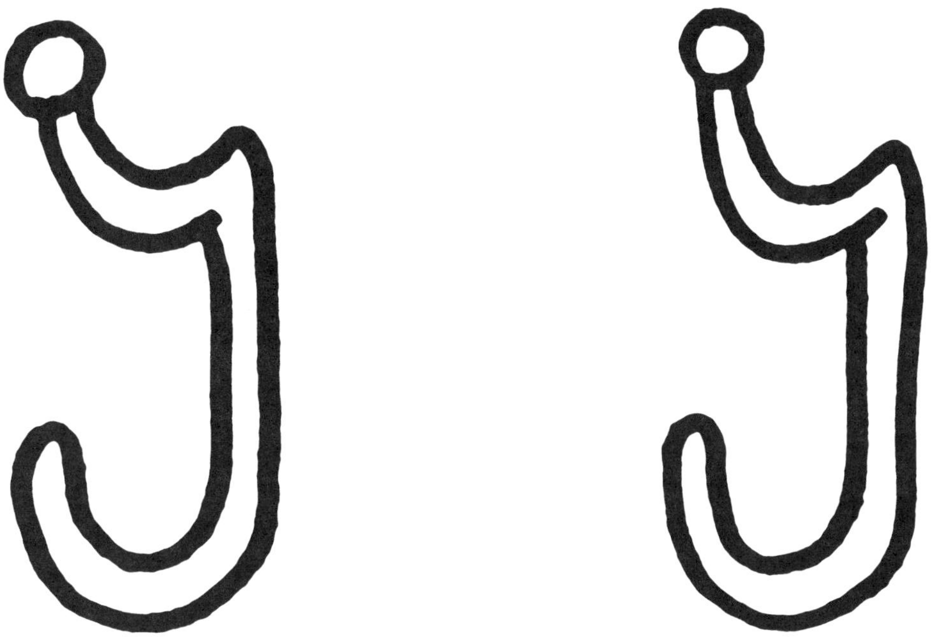

Draw something happy.

You just ordered a delicious meal. What is it?

It's snowing! Fill the sky with snowflakes.

Build a chairlift to carry the skiers up the mountain.

Now send the skiers down!

Draw water shooting from the orca's blowhole.

Draw the tracks made by the ice skater.

Who is getting on the ferry?

What's in the tide pool?

Dig for clams.

Who is climbing the tree?

Fill the forest with trees!

Uh-oh. Mount St. Helens is erupting!

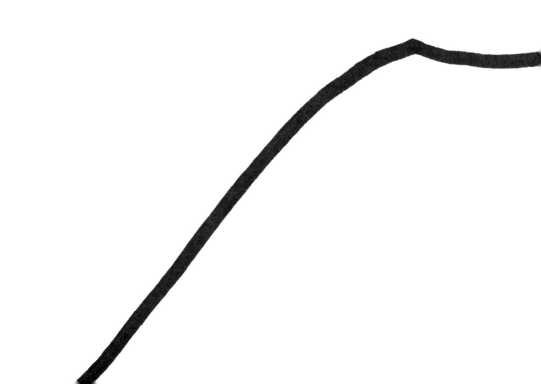

The tugboat is heading into a storm.
Draw the storm.

This is Bangor Naval Base.
Draw a submarine under the water.

How much of the apple is eaten?

Fill the basket with apples.

Draw the animals at the Puyallup Fair.

PETTING
ZOO

Draw all the planes on the aircraft carrier.

Help Debbie and Danny find
the cabin in the woods.

Who is standing on the frozen lake?

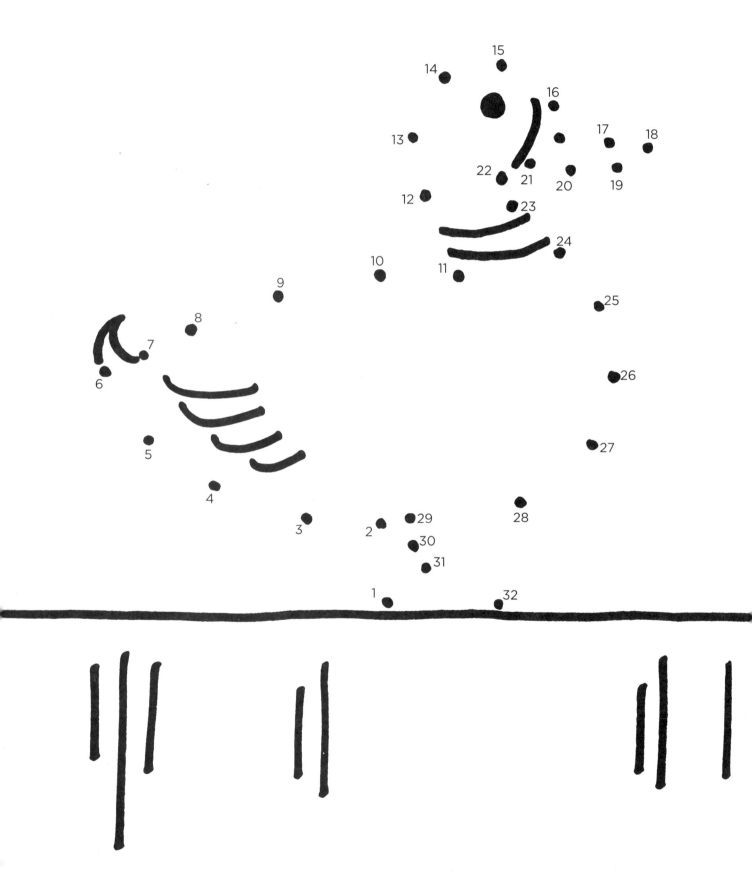